THE SELECTED POEMS OF

T'ao Ch'ien

THE SELECTED POEMS OF

T'ao Ch'ien

TRANSLATED BY DAVID HINTON

COPPER CANYON PRESS

Publication of this book is supported by a grant from the National Endow-
ment for the Arts and a grant from the Lannan Foundation. Additional sup-
port to Copper Canyon Press has been provided by the Andrew W.
Mellon Foundation, the Lila Wallace-Reader's Digest Fund, and the Washington
State Arts Commission. Copper Canyon Press is in residence with Centrum
at Fort Worden State Park.

The translation of this book was supported by grants from the National
Endowment for the Arts and the Vermont Council on the Arts.

Cover: Section one of T'ao Ch'ien's "Drinking Wine."
Calligraphy by Wen Cheng-ming, Ming dynasty. Ink on silk.
Kyoto National Museum.

Library of Congress Cataloging-in Publication Data
T'ao, Ch'ien, 372?–427.
  [Poems. English. Selections]
  The selected poems of T'ao Ch'ien / translated by David Hinton.
    p.   cm.
  ISBN 1-55659-056-3
    1. T'ao, Ch'ien, 372?–427–Translations into English.   I. Hinton,
David, 1954– .   II. Title.
PL2665.T3A245   1993
895.1′12–dc20   93-1635

COPPER CANYON PRESS
Post Office Box 271
Port Townsend, WA 98368

Contents

INTRODUCTION

1. The Work

T'ao Ch'ien (365–427 A.D.), equally well-known by his given name, T'ao Yüan-ming, stands at the head of the great Chinese poetic tradition like a revered grandfather: profoundly wise, self-possessed, quiet, comforting. Although the *Shih Ching (Classic of Poetry)* and *Ch'u Tz'u (Songs of the South)* are the ancient beginnings of the Chinese tradition, T'ao was the first writer to make a poetry of his natural voice and immediate experience, thereby creating the personal lyricism which all major Chinese poets inherited and made their own. And in the quiet resonance of his poetry, a poetry that still speaks today's language, they recognized a depth and clarity of wisdom that seemed beyond them.

T'ao Ch'ien dwelled in the Great Transformation *(ta-hua)*, earth's process of change in which whatever occurs comes "of itself" *(tzu-jan:* literally "self-so," hence "natural" or "spontaneous"). T'ao and his contemporary, Hsieh Ling-yün, are often described as China's first nature poets. But T'ao was much more than a romantic enthralled with the pastoral. He settled on his secluded farm because earth's Great Transformation was perfectly immediate there, because there he could live life as it comes of itself, as it ends of itself. When he spoke of leaving government service and returning to the life of a recluse-farmer, he spoke of "returning to *tzu-jan*." He took comfort in death as an even more complete return, a return to his "native home." Although he grieved over loss and dying because he knew the actual to be all there is, he also knew that whatever is alive, himself included, ceases to be as naturally as it comes to be.

T'ao's return to *tzu-jan* was also a return to self. His poems are suffused with wonder at the elemental fact of consciousness, and at the same time, his poetry of dwelling initiated that intimate sense of belonging to the earth which shapes the Chinese poetic sensibility. For him, identity is itself *tzu-jan*. So, to become a complete and distinctive individual was to become an indistinguishable part of earth's Great Transformation. In a poem not translated in this book, T'ao described this experience of dwelling:

> Vast and majestic, mountains embrace your shadow;
> broad and deep, rivers harbor your voice.

The language T'ao created perfectly mirrors the life he created. He crafted an authentic human voice, and its simple, unassuming surface reveals a rich depth. The great Sung Dynasty (960–1280) poets found this especially impressive. Su Tung-p'o called it "withered and bland": "The outside is withered, but the inside is rich. It seems bland but is actually beautiful." And Huang T'ing-chien said: "When you've just come of age, reading these poems seems like gnawing on withered wood. But reading them after long experience in the world, it seems the decisions of your life were all made in ignorance." If T'ao's poems seem bland, it's because they always begin with the deepest wisdom. They are never animated by the struggle for understanding.

The closest T'ao came to a struggle for understanding was his resolute cultivation of "idleness." Etymologically, the character for idleness *(hsien)* connotes "profound serenity and quietness," its pictographic elements rendering a tree standing alone within the gates to a courtyard or, in its alternate form, moonlight shining through an open door. This idleness is a kind of meditative reveling in *tzu-jan,* a state in which daily life becomes the essence of spiritual practice. Although T'ao's philosophical orientation was primarily Taoist, the Zen community has always revered him because he anticipated many insights of their tradition.

In fact, he became the first in a tradition of Zen figures who stand outside the monastic community, their presence challenging students to free themselves from the unenlightened striving of monastic life by seeing that they are always already enlightened. (The T'ang poet Han Shan is perhaps the most famous such figure.) T'ao lived on the northwest side of Lu Mountain – famous as a site of hermitage because of its great beauty – very close to the most illustrious Buddhist monastery in south China. The monastery abbot Hui-yüan, emphasizing *dhyāna* (meditation), practiced a form of Buddhism which contained the first glimmers of Zen. But even though T'ao maintained close relations with the community there (it is said Hui-yüan tried to recruit him by breaking the rules and serving wine in the monastery), he was never tempted by such extreme, monastic forms of spiritual discipline.

T'ao's workaday idleness would seem to be the very antithesis of monastic disciplines. Indeed, it often takes the form of drinking, a pursuit for which he is justly famous. Although he was certainly capable of getting thoroughly drunk on occasion, drunkenness for T'ao means, as it generally does in Chinese poetry after him, drinking just enough wine to achieve that serene clarity of attention which he calls idleness, a state in which the isolation of a mind imposing distinctions on the world gives way to a sense of identity with the world.

Because T'ao's personal lyricism didn't answer to conventional taste, it received faint praise until the High T'ang literary period (710–780), when Chinese poetry blossomed into its full splendor with such singular poets as Wang Wei, Li Po, and Tu Fu. The admiration poets of that time had for T'ao Ch'ien was a major catalyst in the High T'ang revolution. They recognized in his resolute individuality and authentic human voice an alternative to the lifeless convention of the court tradition which had dominated poetry from T'ao's time to their own. Following the T'ang, the great Sung poets found virtually all of their interests anticipated in the profound simplicity embodied in T'ao's bland voice. And the ability of his work to inspire this kind of admiration has continued through the centuries. If his sensibility seems familiar, it is a measure of his lasting influence. He was the first modern poet, and most modern poetry of the west, having moved beyond its own intellectual heritage, could trace its best tradition back to his lazybones work.

2. *The Life*

The outlines of T'ao Ch'ien's life – his struggle to free himself from the constraints of official life and his eventual commitment to the life of a recluse-farmer, despite poverty and hardship – became one of the central, organizing myths in the Chinese tradition. There is little reliable information about T'ao Ch'ien's life. As less than half of T'ao's 125 surviving poems can be dated, placing them in chronological order presents problems. Nevertheless, the poems in this book are arranged so they recreate the outlines of T'ao's life. Although this involves a considerable amount of guesswork, the legendary status of his life makes it preferable to the haphazard formal arrangement employed in the Chinese texts.

For the educated class in Confucian society, the one honorable alternative to government service was to become a recluse. This might be a Confucian act of protest against an unworthy government, or a Taoist commitment to the spiritual fulfillment of a secluded life. Most often, it was some combination of the two. In T'ao Ch'ien's case, the Taoist impulse was clearly the predominant one. However, T'ao was always a devoted Confucian as well. He entered government service at twenty-nine, and spent most of the next decade in office, which must have involved him in the relentless power struggles of his country's ruthless aristocracy. It is generally agreed that his life and work as a recluse should be read in terms of political protest against an eminently unworthy ruling class. And in spite of its isolated setting, T'ao's poetry is clearly haunted by the country's desperate social situation.

T'ao was born into one of the most chaotic and violent periods of Chinese history. When the Han Dynasty collapsed in 220 A.D., China fell into fragmentation and instability which lasted until the country was again unified under the Sui and T'ang dynasties, over 350 years later. In 317, for the first time in history, "barbarians" took control of the north, the ancient cradle of Chinese civilization, and the Chin Dynasty was forced into the south, a colonial region populated primarily by indigenous, non-Chinese people. The Eastern Chin Dynasty established its capital in Chien-k'ang (present-day Nanjing), but imperial authority was weak and heavily dependent on a handful of very powerful families. Driven to confirm their superiority over the local gentry and the culture supported by "barbarians" in the north, these families created a brief golden age of Chinese culture. But to maintain their wealth and power, they reduced much of the peasantry to virtual slavery on the vast tracts of land which they controlled. This led to widespread discontent and a number of popular rebellions, the most serious of which began during T'ao's years in public service. And in addition to many military campaigns to defend or expand the Chin borders, fierce struggles for power among family factions of the aristocracy led to substantial internal warfare. This situation made official life dangerous and morally compromising for a true Confucian.

T'ao's great-grandfather was a man of considerable importance who played a central role in the founding of the Eastern Chin, but by the time T'ao Ch'ien was born, the T'ao family had become a minor branch of the aristocracy. T'ao's home village was Ch'ai-sang, about six miles southwest of Hsünyang (present day Jiujiang, province of Jiangxi), a provincial capital on the Yangtze River. Dominated by the Lu Mountain complex to the south, it was an especially beautiful area of hills, rivers, and lakes, so T'ao's affection for the family farm is hardly surprising. Coming from an aristocractic family, T'ao was classically educated and was expected to take his proper place in the Confucian order by serving in the government as his father and ancestors had done. This was also the only path to wealth and prestige, both for himself and his family. In 393, when he was twenty-nine, T'ao took a position near his home in the provincial government. But he soon resigned, unable to bear subservience to his overbearing and arrogant superiors. His first wife apparently died at this time, perhaps while giving birth to their first son. A year or two later, T'ao married a woman who is said to have shared his ideals, and by 402, they had four sons. It seems likely that the T'ao family moved to the capital in 395, remaining for six years. T'ao surely would have been working in the central government there, but it isn't clear what position he held, or what part he played in the political intrigues of the time.

In 396, the emperor was strangled, and his five-year-old son was placed on the throne as Emperor An. Emperor An was to reign for twenty-four years, but like his father, he was merely a figurehead controlled by the family factions which arranged his ascension. Huan Hsüan, a general from a competing faction, began building a base of power in the western province where he was governor. In 399, he brought the western part of Chin territory under his control. That same year, the Sun En rebellion broke out in the southeast. This was the largest of the popular rebellions, and it became a major threat to the dynasty when Sun En's forces gained control of the entire southeastern region and moved against the capital.

In 400, T'ao returned from the capital to his home village (the occasion for this book's first poem). This return proved temporary, however, for he soon took a position three hundred miles west in Chiang-ling, on the staff of General Huan Hsüan. As Huan was clearly threatening the Chin government by then, this position may represent a serious compromise of T'ao's integrity. But it's hard to draw any conclusions because so little is known about the situation, and because the emperor's legitimacy was dubious. T'ao took a leave of absence during the spring and summer of 401 to work on his farm, apparently planting a fairly successful crop. He returned to office, only to resign at the end of the year, perhaps because he realized just how dangerous and/or compromising his position was. Throughout his years of official service, T'ao's primary ambition had been to return to the freedom of his farm, and it appears that now, with the spring planting of 402, he finally began living as a recluse-farmer.

He wasn't to leave the farm for three years, a period during which the country underwent a considerable amount of internal warfare. Government forces led by a general named Liu Yü had hardly beaten back the three-year-old Sun En rebellion when, at the end of 403, Huan Hsüan led his armies down the Yangtze from the west, overrunning and surely devastating the Hsün-yang region where T'ao was living, and finally taking control of the capital. Loyal forces regrouped, and again led by Liu Yü, soon defeated Huan Hsüan. Had T'ao remained in Huan's service, he may very well have lost his life in these affairs. Although Liu Yü returned Emperor An to the throne, it was clear that he held the power now.

By 405, the T'ao family was apparently destitute. That spring, desperate for a means of supporting his family, T'ao took a job on the staff of Liu Yü, although the circumstances are unclear. Then in the fall, he took a position as magistrate in P'eng-tse, thirty miles northeast of his home. His resignation of this post after only eighty days was recounted in the early biographies and became a quintessential episode in the T'ao Ch'ien legend:

> Positions meant nothing to him, and he wasn't subservient to high officials. At the end of the year, an inspector was sent to his district. When his assistants told him that he should put on his belt and visit this man, T'ao moaned and said, "I'm not bowing down to some clodhopper for a measly bushel of rice." He untied his seal-ribbon that same day and left office. And to explain how he felt, he wrote "Back Home Again Chant."

"Back Home Again Chant" (p. 32) gives a somewhat contradictory account of what happened, but whatever T'ao's reasons for resigning, this time he left public life for good, even though he had no means of support other than farm work, which had proven painfully unreliable. Although he received several requests to serve in the government, T'ao farmed in the Ch'ai-sang/Hsün-yang area until his death twenty-two years later.

During this time, the country's militarism continued with the same devastating results. Incessant infighting among factions of the aristocracy persisted, sometimes involving battles between substantial armies. In 410, Sun En's successor led an army down the Yangtze in a campaign against the capital, plundering the countryside and occupying the Hsün-yang region until he was finally beaten back. And in 416, Liu Yü led a year-long campaign which succeeded in recapturing north China from the "barbarians," only to lose it again a year later. Through it all, Liu steadily increased his power until finally, in 420, after disposing of Emperor An and his successor, he declared himself emperor of his own Liu-Sung Dynasty. But his health was poor, and he died two years later. Thereupon, in addition to renewed hostilities with the "barbarians" of the north, the aristocracy's deadly infighting began anew. Although we know T'ao maintained close relations with high officials of the new dynasty, it is said that he protested Liu Yü's usurpation by adopting the name *Ch'ien,* meaning "in hiding," hence: The Recluse T'ao. In the end, it was his life as a poor recluse-farmer that was the most important political fact about T'ao's career: by living the fate of the common people who always pay such a terrible price for the whims of those in power, and wresting such sufficiency from that fate, T'ao made his most private poems intensely political statements.

Indeed, T'ao wrote a brief autobiographical sketch imitating the form used for biographies in the *Shih Chi (Records of the Grand Historian)* and the *Han Shu (History of the Former Han),* where the lives of great political figures of old are recorded. But whereas the ancient histories recorded the official positions and historic deeds of their illustrious subjects, T'ao describes his uneventful life of poverty and idleness. By using this form, T'ao asserts the essential nobility of his life and, at the same time, invests the piece with a sure sense of farce:

Biography of Master Five-Willows

No one knows where he came from. His given and literary names are also a mystery. But we know there were five willows growing beside his house, which is why he used this name. At peace in idleness, rarely speaking, he had no longing for fame or fortune. He loved to read books, and yet never puzzled over their profound insights. But whenever he came upon some realization, he was so pleased that he forgot to eat.

He was a wine-lover by nature, but couldn't afford it very often. Everyone knew this, so when they had wine, they'd call him over. And when he drank, it was always bottoms-up. He'd be drunk in no time; then he'd go back home, alone and with no regrets over where things were going.

In the loneliness of his meager wall, there was little shelter from wind and sun. His short coat was patched and sewn. And made from gourd and split bamboo, his cup and bowl were empty as often as Yen Hui's. But he kept writing poems to amuse himself, and they show something of who he was. He went on like this, forgetting all gain and loss, until he came naturally to his end.

In appraisal we say: Ch'ien Lou said *Don't make yourself miserable agonizing over impoverished obscurity, and don't wear yourself out scrambling for money and honor.* Doesn't that describe this kind of man perfectly? He'd just get merrily drunk and write poems to cheer himself up. He must have lived in the most enlightened and ancient of times. If it wasn't Emperor Wu-huai's reign, surely it was Ko-t'ien's.

THE SELECTED POEMS OF

T'ao Ch'ien

RETURNING TO MY OLD HOME

We moved to the capital in another time,
it seems, only leaving for home after

six years. Today, our first day back,
I grieve. Sad things are everywhere now.

Terraced fields remain, still unchanged,
but in the village, entire houses simply

vanished. And out walking, I find old
neighbors here mostly dead. I take my

time, looking for what lasted, traces
I linger over jealously. Day after day,

life's hundred years all flowing illusion,
hot and cold hurry each other away.

Facing old fears the Great Transformation
will end me before *ch'i*'s breath leaves,

I let go – let go and forget it all.
A little wine still brings me to life.

After Liu Ch'ai-Sang's Poem

I'd long felt these mountains and lakes
beckoning, and wouldn't have thought twice,

but my family and friends couldn't bear
talk of living apart. Then one lucky day

a strange feeling came over me, and I left,
walking-stick in hand, for my western farm.

No one was going back home: on those outland
roads, farm after farm lay in empty ruins,

but our thatch hut's already good as ever,
and you'd think our new fields had been

tended for years. When valley winds turn
cold, spring wine eases hunger and work,

and though it isn't strong, just baby-girl
wine, it's better than nothing for worry.

Distant – as months and years pass away here,
the bustling world's racket grows distant.

Plowing and weaving provide all we use.
Who needs anything more? Away, ever away

into this hundred-year life and beyond,
my story and I vanish together like this.

Home Again Among Gardens and Fields

I

Nothing like the others, even as a child,
rooted in a love for hills and mountains,

I fell into their net of dust, that one
departure a blunder lasting thirteen years.

But a tethered bird longs for its forest,
a pond fish its deep waters. So now, my

land out on the south edge cleared, I
nurture simplicity among gardens and fields,

home again. I've got nearly two acres here,
and four or five rooms in my thatch hut.

Elms and willows shade the eaves out back,
and in front, peach and plum spread wide.

Distant – village people lost in distant
haze, kitchen smoke hangs above wide-open

country. Here, dogs bark deep in back roads,
and roosters crow from mulberry treetops.

No confusion within the gate, no dust,
my empty home harbors idleness to spare.

Back again: after so long in that trap,
I've returned to all that comes of itself.

2

So little out here ever involves people.
Visitors to our meager lane rare, my

bramble gate closed all day, this empty
home cuts dust-filled thoughts short.

And day after day, coming and going
on overgrown paths, I meet neighbors

without confusion: we only talk about
how the crops are doing, nothing more.

Mine grow taller each day, and my fields
grow larger, but I can't stop worrying:

come frost or sleet, and it all falls
into tatters, like so much tangled brush.

3

I planted beans below South Mountain.
A few sprouted, then brush took over.

I get up early to clear weeds, and
shouldering my hoe, return by moonlight.

The path narrow, the brush and trees
thick, evening dew pierces my clothes.

But they're not too wet—just damp
enough it reminds me never to resist.

4

Years never wandering mountains and lakes
gone, elated again amid forests and fields,

I take children by the hand and set out
through woods and abandoned farmlands.

Soon, we're walking around aimlessly among
gravemounds and houses deserted long ago,

their wells and brick stoves still standing
here among broken-down bamboo and mulberry.

Someone is gathering firewood, so I ask
where these people are, all these people.

Turning toward me, he replies *Once you're
dead and gone, nothing's left*. They say

a single generation and, court or market,
every face is new. It's true, of course.

Life is its own mirage of change. It ends
vanished, returned into nothing. What else?

AFTER KUO CHU-PU'S POEMS

I

Trees thick and full gathering pure
midsummer shade out front, and wind

coming in its season, gentle gusts
opening my robe – I live life apart

here. Cultivating idleness, I roam
koto strings and books all day long,

our vegetable garden full of plenty,
last year's grain holding out well.

In making a living, we gain by limits.
Wanting nothing beyond enough, nothing,

I grind millet, make up a lovely wine,
and when it's ripe, ladle it out myself.

Our son plays beside me. Too young
to speak, he keeps trying new sounds.

All this brings back such joy I forget
glittering careers. White clouds drift

endless skies. I watch. Why all that
reverent longing for ancient times?

2

We had warm, wet weather all spring. Now,
white autumn is clear and cold. Dew frozen,

drifting mists gone, bottomless heavens
open over this vast landscape of clarity,

and mountains stretch away, their towering
peaks an unearthly treasure of distance.

Fragrant chrysanthemums ablaze in woodlands
blooming, green pines lining the clifftops:

isn't this the immaculate heart of beauty,
this frost-deepened austerity? Sipping wine,

I think of recluse masters. A century away,
I nurture your secrets. Your true nature

eludes me here, but taken by quiet, I can
linger this exquisite moon out to the end.

Early Spring, *Kuei* Year of the Hare, Thinking of Ancient Farmers

I

Though I knew *southern fields* in song
long ago, I'd never walked out into them.

Invariably hungry, Yen perfected wisdom,
but how can I ignore spring breaking out

here? At dawn, loading up my cart and
setting out, I already feel far away.

Birds sing, celebrating the new season.
Cool winds bring blessings in abundance,

and in these distances empty of people,
bamboo crowds country paths. Now I see

why that farmer laughing at Confucius
lived so far away and never went back.

My way seems childish to the world-wise,
but what I nurture here never grows thin.

2

He's still our master teacher, and right
to say *Worry about the Way, not hunger,*

but that's far beyond my reach, so I'll
make this long hard work wisdom instead.

Plow in hand, the season's task my delight,
I smile and coax the others on. Distant

wind sweeping in across fields, delicate
seedlings also wonder at this fresh life.

Though I'm not sure of a good harvest,
there's joy enough in fieldwork itself,

rest enough after spring planting. Here,
where passersby never stop to ask the Way,

we walk home at dusk. After sharing wine,
simple thanks to neighbors, I chant poems

late, then close my brushwood gate. I'll
take this farmland life anytime, anytime.

In Reply to Liu Ch'ai-Sang

In a meager home, guests rare, I often
forget I'm surrounded by turning seasons.

And now falling leaves fill courtyard
emptiness, I grow sad, realizing it's

autumn already. Fresh sunflower thickets
fill north windows. Sweet grains in south

fields ripen. Though I'm far from happy
today, I know next year may never come.

Get the kids together, I tell my wife,
it's the perfect day for a nice long walk.

Written in the 12th Month, *Kuei* Year of the Hare, for My Cousin Ching-Yüan

At this distant, bramble-woven gate, my
wandering come to rest, the world and I

let each other go. Not a soul in sight.
At dusk, who knows my gate sat closed

all day? This year-end wind bitter cold,
falling snow a thick, day-long shroud,

there isn't a trace of sound. I listen,
eyes aching from all this white clarity.

Cold seeping inside robes, cups and bowls
rarely agreeing to be set out for meals,

it's all desolation in this empty house,
nothing anywhere to keep our spirits up.

Roaming through thousand-year-old books,
I meet timeless exemplars. I'll never

reach their high principles, though I've
somehow mastered *resolute in privation,*

and there's no chance renown will redeem
this poverty. But I'm no fool for coming

here. I send findings beyond all words:
who could understand this bond we share?

BEGGING FOOD

Hunger came and drove me out. No
idea where I'd end up, I went on

and on, and coming to this village,
knocked at some door. Seeing in my

senseless muttering why I'd come,
you gave all I needed, and more:

we chatted on into evening, pouring
cups of wine we downed in no time,

and savoring the joy of new friends,
we chanted old poems and wrote new.

You're kind as that woman who fed
half-starved Han Hsin. But I'll never

rise to glory, never have anything but
gifts from the grave to send in thanks.

Written on Passing Through Ch'ü-o, Newly Appointed to Advise Liu Yü's Normalization Army

I came of age out beyond all their affairs,
taking comfort in *koto* and books. My robe

simple, I delighted in life coming of itself,
and though often hungry, spent years at ease.

Then that sad surprise came, and I turned
onto the well-traveled road, ending it all.

Packed by morning, I left my walking-stick,
and suddenly my fields and gardens were far

away. Alone, vanishing boat drifting away,
thoughts weaving endless threads of return,

who could pretend this journey won't be long,
a thousand up-and-down miles long, and more?

Eyes haggard from strange rivers and roads,
I dream of my life among mountains and lakes.

For now, birds free among high clouds may
put me to shame, and fish roaming streams,

but rooted deep in my native mindfulness,
I've never been taken in by appearance:

trusting the movement of change, I'll return
after all to that home solitude builds.

After an Ancient Poem

Distant, on this distant, hundred-foot high
tower, four horizons open into plain view,

open home at night for returning clouds
and a room for birds in morning flight.

Rivers and mountains filling sight, a lone
plain stretches endlessly away. Long ago,

illustrious men of renown, in noble-hearted
gallantry, made their battleground here,

and in a morning, their hundred-year lives
over, they all went to the grave together.

Clear-cut by those needing pine and cypress,
looming gravemounds swell and dip into one

another. There's no one to tend crumbling
tombs. And where are those wandering spirits

now? Such glory is to be prized, no doubt,
but we'll always mourn the wounds later.

We were destitute. I worked hard farming, but we never had enough: the house was full of kids, and the rice-jar always empty. And though people have made their living like this for countless generations, I never quite caught on, so everyone kept pushing me to find government work. Finally I decided they were right, but had no idea where to begin. Before long I had to do some traveling, and some important people I met seemed impressed by me. Then, when my uncle took an interest in our bitter poverty, I found myself appointed to office in a small town. At that time, since the land was still full of trouble, I was leery about serving far away. But P'eng-tse was only thirty miles from here, and the receipts from government fields were enough to keep me in wine, so I took the job. The first few days went well enough; then all I wanted was to be home with my family again. Why the sudden change of heart? My nature comes of itself. It isn't something you can force into line. Hunger and cold may cut deep, but turning on myself that way felt like a sickness. Serving the public good, I was nothing more than a mouth and belly serving themselves. Seeing this, and thinking of the ideals I'd always held, I was sad and utterly ashamed of my fine public spirit. And yet, I still thought I should hold out until next year's harvest before packing up and slipping away in the night. But soon my younger sister, Chang's wife, died in Wu-chang, and forgetting everything in the rush to get there, I escaped, leaving my duties behind. After holding office more than eighty days, from mid-autumn into winter, I turned what happened into my heart's content.

My piece is called *Back Home Again,* and this preface was written in the 11th month, *Yi* year of the snake.

Back home –
with fields and gardens all weeds back home,
how can I stay here, my heart a slave to the body?
Why live this dismal life, this lonely grief?
You can't argue with what's been done, I know,
but the future's there to be made. Not too far
gone down this road of delusion, I can see
where I'm right today, yesterday I was wrong.

Far from home, the boat rocking on gentle
swells, my robe snaps in billowing winds.
Asking travelers how the road ahead is,
I wonder how morning light can be so dim,
but seeing our house, suddenly
happy, I break into a run.
Servants greet me gleefully,
and my kids there at the gate.
Our three paths are grown over,
but pines and chrysanthemums
survived. And taking everyone
inside, I find wine waiting.
Pouring a cup from the winejar, I smile, happy
to see these courtyard trees. At the window
my presumptions drift away south. How easily
content I am in this cramped little place.
Here, garden strolls bring joy day after day:
our gate always closed, propped on my old-folk's
walking-stick, I go a little ways, then rest,

and turning my head, look far away. Clouds
leaving mountain peaks drift without a thought,
and tired of flight, birds think of return.
At sunset, light fading slowly away, I linger
fondly over a lone pine, nowhere I'd rather be.

Back home again –
O let me keep to myself, my wandering ended.
Let the world and I give each other up.
If I left again, what would I go looking for?
It's loving family voices that make me happy,
koto and books that keep worried grief away.
And farmers here tell me spring has arrived. Soon,
there'll be work out in the western fields.
Sometimes in a covered cart,
sometimes rowing a lone boat –
I'll search out sheltered streams and quiet pools,
follow mountain paths up through the hills.
Trees revel in the joy of their lavish blossoms,
and murmuring springs flow again. In these
ten thousand things, each following its season
away perfectly, I touch that repose in which
life ends, done and gone.
This form I am in the world can't last much longer.
Why not let things carry my heart away with them?
What good is it, agonizing over the way things are going?
Getting rich isn't what I want. And who
expects to end in some celestial village?
My dream is to walk out all alone into a lovely

morning – maybe stop to pull weeds in the garden,
maybe climb East Ridge and chant, settling into
my breath, or sit writing poems beside a clear
stream. I'll ride change back to my final home,
rejoicing in heaven's way. How can it ever fail me?

Untitled

I couldn't want another life. This is my
true calling, working fields and mulberries

with my own two hands. I've never failed it,
and still, against hunger and cold, there's

only hull and chaff. I'm not asking for more
than a full stomach. All I want is enough

common rice, heavy clothes for winter and
open-weaves for the summer heat – nothing

more. But I haven't even managed that. O,
it can leave you stricken so with grief.

And character is fate. If you're simple-
minded in life, its ways elude you. That's

how it is. Nothing can change it. But then,
I'll delight in even a single cup of wine.

TURNING SEASONS

Turning Seasons is about wandering in late spring. Spring clothes are all made, and everything in sight is tranquil. I wander beside my shadow, alone, my heart a blend of delight and grief.

1

Turning seasons turning wildly
away, morning's majestic calm

unfolds. Out in spring clothes,
I cross eastern fields. A few

clouds linger, sweeping mountains
clean. Gossamer mist blurs open

skies. Feeling the south wind,
young grain ripples like wings.

2

Boundless, the lake's immaculate
skin boundless, I rinse myself

clean. The view all distance,
all distance inciting delight,

I look deep. They say if you're
content you're satisfied easily

enough. Raising this winecup, I
smile, taken by earth's own joy.

37

3

Gazing midstream, longing for
that clear Yi River, I see sage

ancients there, taking in spring
and returning carefree in song.

What exquisite calm. I'd join
them in a moment, but nothing's

left of their world now, only
sorrow and distance. No way back,

4

I'm home day-in day-out, taking
things easy. Herbs and flowers

grow in rows. Trees and bamboo
gather shade. My *koto* is tuned

clear, and a half-jar of thick
wine waits. Unable to reach that

golden age Huang and T'ang ruled,
I inhabit who I am sad and alone.

FORM, SHADOW, SPIRIT

Rich or poor, wise or foolish, people are all busy clinging jealously to their lives. And it's such delusion. So, I've presented as clearly as I could the sorrows of Form and Shadow. Then, to dispel those sorrows, Spirit explains occurrence coming naturally of itself. Anyone who's interested in such things will see what I mean.

1 *Form Addresses Shadow*

Heaven and earth last. They'll never end.
Mountains and rivers know no seasons,

and there's a timeless law plants and trees
follow: frost then dew, vigor then ruin.

They call us earth's most divine and wise
things, but we alone are never as we are

again. One moment we appear in this world,
and the next, we vanish, never to return.

And who notices one person less? Family?
Friends? They only remember when some

everyday little thing you've left behind
pushes grief up to their eyes in tears.

I'm no immortal. I can't just soar away
beyond change. There's no doubt about it,

death's death. Once you see that, you'll
see that turning down drinks is for fools.

2 Shadow Replies

Who can speak of immortality when simply
staying alive makes such sad fools of us?

We long for those peaks of the immortals,
but they're far-off, and roads trail away

early. Coming and going together, we've
always shared the same joys and sorrows.

Resting in shade, we may seem unrelated,
but living out in the sun, we never part.

This togetherness isn't forever, though.
Soon, we'll smother in darkness. The body

can't last, and all memory of us also ends.
It sears the five feelings. But in our

good works, we bequeath our love through
generations. How can you spare any effort?

Though it may be true wine dispels sorrow,
how can such trifles ever compare to this?

3 *Spirit Answers*

The Great Potter never hands out favors.
These ten thousand things thrive each

of themselves alone. If humans rank with
heaven and earth, isn't it because of me?

And though we're different sorts of things
entirely, we've been inseparable since

birth, together through better and worse,
and I've always told you what I thought.

The Three Emperors were the wisest of men,
but where are they now? And loving his

eight-hundred-year life, old P'eng-tsu
wanted to stay on here, but he too set out.

Young and old die the same death. When it
comes, the difference between sage and fool

vanishes. Drinking every day may help you
forget, but won't it bring an early grave?

And though good works may bring lasting
joy, who will sing your praise? Listen –

it's never-ending analysis that wounds us.
Why not circle away in the seasons, adrift

on the Great Transformation, riding its vast
swells without fear or delight? Once your

time comes to an end, you end: not another
moment lost to all those lonely worries.

SCOLDING MY SONS

My temples covered all in white, I'm
slack-muscled and loose-skinned for good

now. And though I do have five sons,
not one of them prizes paper and brush.

A-shu is already twice eight, and who's
ever equaled him for sheer laziness?

A-hsüan is fifteen, time studies began,
but he's immune to words and ideas.

Yung and Tuan are both thirteen now,
and they can't even add six and seven.

And T'ung-tzu, who's almost nine, does
nothing but forage pears and chestnuts.

If this is heaven's way, I'll offer it
that stuff in the cup. It needs a drink.

9/9, *CHI* YEAR OF THE ROOSTER

In all its reckless leisure, autumn begins
its end. Cold – the dew-charged wind cold,

vines will blossom no more. Our courtyard
trees have spent themselves: they stand

empty. Dingy air washed clean, clear sky
heightens the distant borders of heaven,

and now mourning cicadas have gone silent,
geese call out beneath gossamer clouds.

The ten thousand changes follow each other
away – so why shouldn't living be hard?

And everyone dies. It's always been true,
I know, but thinking of it still leaves me

grief-torn. How can I reach my feelings?
A little thick wine, and I'm soon pleased

enough. A thousand years may be beyond me,
but I can turn this morning into forever.

9TH MONTH, *KENG* YEAR OF THE DOG, EARLY RICE HARVESTED IN THE WEST FIELD

For a life returned to the Way, you
begin with food and clothes. Who can

ignore what we need most, and still
hope to find earth's own composure?

The task begun in early spring drags on,
but then I see another year's harvest,

go out at dawn and, after an easy
day's work, haul grain home at dusk.

Now, heavy dew and frost blankets this
hill-country, and wind is turning cold.

How could farm life be anything but
bitter? No one avoids these troubles,

but my arms and legs are so tired they
ache. I couldn't bear any more worries.

I wash, then sit out beneath the eaves,
relaxed, cheered by wine. How far away,

hermits Chü and Ni a thousand years away,
and we're of one mind. All I want is

more of the same, much more. Working
your own fields is no cause for lament.

Thinking of Impoverished Ancients

I

Ten thousand things, and yet nothing
without refuge but lone cloud. Into dusk –

vanishing into empty skies, into dusk,
when will last light ever grace it again?

Flushed dawn sky breaking through last
night's fog, birds take flight together:

they venture carefully from the woods,
and wing home again well before evening.

Hoarding strength and guarding life apart,
how could anyone avoid hunger and cold?

If there's no one left who understands,
then that's that: what would you mourn?

2

Bitter cold. The year ending like this,
I sun on the front porch, my coat closed.

There's nothing left of our south garden,
and dead limbs fill orchards to the north.

I try the ricejar: not a grain. I peer
inside the stove: no sign even of smoke.

It's late afternoon, classics piled nearby,
but I can't read in peace. This idle life –

it's not like Confucius in Ch'en, people
half-starved, but they're angry here, too,

and say so. Is there any solace? All those
ancients living this same enlightened life?

WE'VE MOVED

I

I first wanted to live in South Village
long ago – not for its *ch'i*-sited homes,

but for its simple-hearted people, people
who'd make mornings and evenings pure

joy. And now, after years of dreaming,
it's finally happened. We're poor, but

who needs a spacious house? If it covers
our beds and mats, that's plenty enough.

Neighbors stop in every now and again,
our debates nothing but old times, small-

talk. And we delight in strange poems
together, explaining lines that elude us.

2

Spring and fall offer countless lovely
days to climb mountains and write new

poems. At each gate, greetings rise,
and if there's wine, it's ladled out.

After a day's work, we each return home
alone to relax. Or suddenly, friends

coming to mind, we dress up and go out,
and can't get enough talk or laughter.

There's no better life, and no chance
I'll leave. Though it's true we can't

live without food and clothes, working
these fields will never shortchange me.

DRINKING WINE

There's little to enjoy in this idle life, and already the nights are
growing longer. I happen to have some illustrious wine, so I
don't let an evening pass without dipping some out. I down a
few cups alone, facing my shadow, and suddenly I'm drunk
again, scribbling out lines all at once to amuse myself. This be-
gan some time ago, so by now I've got lots of ink-covered pa-
per. Though there's no order to them, I thought the poems
might be entertaining, so I've asked an old friend to write out a
clean copy for me.

I

Vigor and ruin never stay put. Here,
there – all things share in this alike.

Farming melons, how could Shao live
anything like that royal life he lost?

Cold dies into hot, hot into cold.
It's our Way, too. Nothing is immune.

But those who understand it live their
lives worry-free. Whenever chance

brings along a jar of wine, they'll
take it, all delight as night falls.

2

The Way's been in ruins a thousand
years. People all hoard their hearts

away: so busy scrambling for esteemed
position, they'd never touch wine.

But whatever makes living precious
occurs in this one life, and this

life never lasts. It's startling,
sudden as lightning. These hundred

years offer all abundance: Take it!
What more could you make of yourself?

3

I live in town without all that racket
horses and carts stir up, and you wonder

how that could be. Wherever the mind
dwells apart is itself a distant place.

Picking chrysanthemums at my east fence,
far off, I see South Mountain: mountain

air lovely at dusk, birds in flight
returning home. All this means something,

something absolute. Whenever I start
explaining it, I've forgotten the words.

4

Colors infusing autumn chrysanthemums
exquisite, I pick dew-bathed petals,

float them on that forget-your-cares
stuff. Even my passion for living apart

soon grows distant. I'm alone, but after
that first cup, the winejar pours itself.

Everything at rest, dusk: a bird calls,
returning to its forest home. Chanting,

I settle into my breath. Somehow, on this
east veranda, I've found my life again.

5

In the east garden, there's a green pine
overgrown with brush, its beauty shrouded.

When frost comes, killing everything else,
its majestic, towering branches appear.

No one noticed it among the trees, but now
it stands alone, they're amazed. My winejar

slung from a cold branch, I keep looking
far away. Here, in the midst of this

dreamed sleight-of-hand, what could ever
tangle me in the world's tether of dust?

6

People praise Yen's benevolence, say
Jung mastered the Way. So often empty,

one died young. Always hungry, the other
lived to a ripe old age. Their names

outlived death, but they eked out such
haggard lives. And renown means nothing

once we're dead and gone. Simple-hearted
contentment – it's all that matters.

We coddle thousand-gold selves, but
we're only guests: change soon takes

our treasure. Why not naked burial?
People need to get beyond old ideas.

7

Old friends share my weakness. They come
bringing full winejars, and spreading

brambleweave mats, we sit beneath pines.
After a few rounds, we're drunk again,

esteemed elders yakking away all at once
and losing track of who's pouring when.

Soon, that sense of knowing I exist gone,
nothing's precious, nothing worthless.

All distance, we're lost where we are. O,
this wine hides such bottomless flavors.

8

Too poor to hire help, we're being taken
over by a wilderness tangle of trees. All

silence, birds drifting clear skies and
isolate silence, there's no sign of others.

Time and space go on forever, but who
lives even to a hundred? Months and years

tighten, bustling each other away, and my
hair was already turning white long ago.

If we don't give up failure and success,
that promise we hold just turns to regret.

WINE STOP

I've stopped. Here in town, where idleness
coming of itself stopped my far wandering,

I've stopped sitting anywhere but deep shade
and stopped going out my brambleweave gate.

Cuisine stops with mallow. And kids—I've
stopped enjoying anything so much as kids.

I'd drunk nonstop my whole life through,
knowing it all felt wrong when I stopped.

I tried stopping at dusk, but couldn't sleep,
and stopping at dawn, I couldn't get up.

Day after day, I'd nearly start stopping,
but it never stopped promising metabolic

disaster. All I knew was it hurt to stop.
I couldn't see how much stopping offered,

but this morning, the virtues of stopping
clear at last, I managed a full, dead stop.

Setting out from this wine stop, I'll soon
stop by that island of immortals, where

youth stops stopping on pure faces. I won't
stop now for countless thousands of years.

WANDERING AT HSIEH CREEK

On the 5th day of the 1st month, *Hsin* year of the ox, the air was fresh and clear, and the earth lovely in its idleness, so I went out with two or three neighbors to wander at Hsieh Creek. There, sitting beside full-flowing water, we gazed toward the Tseng Cliffs. At dusk, bream and carp started leaping, their scales flashing. Gulls climbed into the still air, where they glided back and forth. Those southern mountains have been famous forever; they don't need any more songs of praise. But the Tseng Cliffs rose from the water with their own distant, isolate beauty. Having a name we treasure, they made us think of the K'un-lun Mountains, peaks of immortality. Not satisfied with the pleasure of gazing at them, we began writing poems. And suddenly spirit-wounded, we lamented the way days and months pass away, for nothing can hold our years back.

We wanted these poems to mark the occasion for us, so we each added our age and home village.

> This new year makes it fifty suddenly
> gone. Thinking of life's steady return
>
> to rest cuts deep, driving me to spend
> all morning wandering. And now, air
>
> fresh and sky clear, I sit with friends
> beside a stream flowing far away. Here,
>
> striped bream weave the gentle current,
> and calling, gulls rise over the lazy

valley. Eyes wandering distant waters,
straining, I make out Tseng Hill: it's

meager compared to K'un-lun's majestic
peaks, but nothing in sight rivals it.

Taking the winejar, I pour out a round,
and we start offering brimful toasts.

Who knows where today leads, or whether
things will ever be like this again?

After a few cups, my heart's far away,
and I've forgotten thousand-year sorrows:

ranging to the limit of this morning's
joy, it isn't tomorrow I'm looking for.

TOGETHER, WE ALL GO OUT UNDER THE CYPRESS TREES IN THE CHOU FAMILY BURIAL-GROUNDS

Today's skies are perfect for a clear
flute and singing *koto*. And touched

this deeply by those laid under these
cypress trees, how could we neglect joy?

Clear songs drift away anew. Emerald wine
starts pious faces smiling. Not knowing

what tomorrow brings, it's exquisite
exhausting whatever I feel here and now.

Steady Rain, Drinking Alone

Life soon returns to nothing. The ancients
all said it circles away like this. And if

Sung and Ch'iao ever lived in this world
without dying, where are they now? Still,

my old neighbor swears his wine makes you
immortal, so I try a little. Soon, those

hundred feelings grow distant. Another cup,
and suddenly I've forgotten heaven. O,

how could heaven be anywhere but here?
Stay true to the actual, yielding to all things,

and in a moment, unearthly cloud-cranes
carrying immortals beyond all eight horizons

return. Since I first embraced solitude,
I've struggled through forty years. And yet,

in this body long since lost to change,
my thoughts remain, quite silent after all.

In the 6th Month, *Wu* Year of the Horse, Fire Broke Out

In our thatched hut on a meager lane, I'd
eluded illustrious guests. But a midsummer

wind hit, wild and steady, and suddenly
house and trees – everything caught fire.

Not a roof anywhere survived, so we took
shelter here, on this boat outside our gate.

Fruits and vegetables are growing back now,
though the panicked birds haven't returned.

Boundless – early autumn night boundlessly
open, an almost-full moon drifts perfectly

alone. Out in this night, thoughts far-off,
a single glance gathers all nine heavens.

I embraced solitude young, my hair scarcely
tied-up. And now, forty years are suddenly

gone. The body passes, an echo of change,
but my lone spirit, at home in idleness,

remains – pure and enduring, a singular
element unto itself and harder than jade.

I think of that world Tung-hu ruled, where
surplus grain lay overnight in the fields

and carefree people thumped full bellies,
where they rose at dawn and returned each

evening to sleep. An utter stranger to
such things, I go on watering my garden.

AN IDLE 9/9 AT HOME

Spending an idle 9/9 at home, I think fondly of how the day's name sounds like it's saying *ever and ever*. Autumn chrysanthemums fill the dooryard. But without wine, their blossoms promising *ever*-lasting life are useless, so I trust my feelings to words.

Life too short for so many lasting desires,
people adore immortality. When the months

return to this day of promise, everyone
fondly hears *ever and ever* in its name.

Warm winds have ended. Now, dew ice-cold,
stars blaze in clear skies. And though

the swallows have gone, taking their shadows,
calling geese keep arriving. Wine dispels

worries by the hundred, and chrysanthemums
keep us from the ruins of age. But if you

live in a bramble hut, helplessly watching
these turning seasons crumble – what then?

My empty winejar shamed by a dusty cup, this
cold splendor of blossoms opens for itself

alone. I tighten my robe and sing to myself,
idle, overwhelmed by each memory. So many

joys to fill a short stay. I'll take my time
here. It is whole. How could it be any less?

It's early summer. Everything's lush.
Our house set deep among broad trees,

birds delight in taking refuge here.
I too love this little place. And now

the plowing and planting are finished,
I can return to my books again and read.

Our meager lane nowhere near well-worn
roads, most old friends turn back. Here,

I ladle out spring wine with pleasure,
and pick vegetables out in the garden.

And coming in from the east, thin rain
arrives on a lovely breeze. My eyes

wander *Tales of Emperor Mu,* float along
on *Mountains and Seas* pictures. . . .

Look around. All time and space within
sight – if not here, where will joy come?

Cha Festival Day

Seeing off the year's final day, windblown
snow can't slow warm weather. Already,

at our gate planted with plum and willow,
there's a branch flaunting lovely blossoms.

When I chant, words come clear. And in wine
I touch countless distances. So much that

still eludes me – who knows how much when
there's such unearthly Chang Mountain song?

Seeing Guests Off at Governor Wang's

Autumn days bitter cold, the hundred plants
already in ruins – now footsteps-in-frost

season has come, we climb this tower to
offer those returning home our farewell.

In cold air shrouding mountains and lakes,
forever rootless, clouds drift. And all

those islands carry our thoughts far away,
across threatening wind and water. Here,

we watch night fall, delighting in fine food,
our lone sorrow this talk of separation.

Morning birds return for the night. A looming
sun bundles its last light away. Our roads

part here: you vanish, we remain. Sad,
we linger and look back – eyes seeing off

your boat grown distant, hearts settled in
whatever comes of the ten thousand changes.

During the T'ai-yüan years [376–397 A.D.] of the Chin Dynasty, there was a man in Wu-ling who caught fish for a living. One day he went up a stream, and soon didn't know how far he'd gone. Suddenly, he came upon a peach orchard in full bloom. For hundreds of feet, there was nothing but peach trees crowding in over the banks. And in the confusion of fallen petals, there were lovely, scented flowers. The fisherman was amazed. Wanting to see how far the orchard went, he continued on.

The trees ended at the foot of a mountain, where a spring fed the stream from a small cave. It seemed as if there might be a light inside, so the fisherman left his boat and stepped in. At first, the cave was so narrow he could barely squeeze through. But he kept going and, after a few dozen feet, it opened out into broad daylight. There, on a plain stretching away, austere houses were graced with fine fields and lovely ponds. Dikes and paths crossed here and there among mulberries and bamboo. Roosters and dogs called back and forth. Coming and going in the midst of all this, there were men and women tending the fields. Their clothes were just like those worn by the people outside. And whether they were old with white hair or children in pigtails, they were all happy and of themselves content.

When they saw the fisherman, they were terribly surprised and asked where he had come from. Once he had answered all their questions, they insisted on taking him back home. And soon, they had set out wine and killed chickens for dinner. When the others in the village heard about this man, they all came to ask about him. They told him how, long ago, to escape those years of turmoil during the Ch'in Dynasty

[221 – 207 B.C.], the village ancestors gathered their wives and children, and with their neighbors came to this distant place. And never leaving, they'd kept themselves cut-off from the people outside ever since. So now they wondered what dynasty it was. They'd never heard of the Han, let alone Wei or Chin. As the fisherman carefully told them everything he knew, they all sighed in sad amazement. Soon, each of the village families had invited him to their house, where they also served wine and food.

After staying for some days, the fisherman prepared to leave these people. As he was going, they said *There's no need to tell the people outside*. He returned to his boat and started back, careful to remember each place along the way.

When he got back home, he went to tell the prefect what had happened, and the prefect sent some men to retrace the route with him. They tried to follow the landmarks he remembered, but they were soon lost and finally gave up the search.

Liu Tzu-chi, who lived in Nan-yang, was a recluse of great honor and esteem. When he heard about this place, he joyfully prepared to go there. But before he could, he got sick and passed away. Since then, no one's asked the Way.

Ch'in's First Emperor ravaged the sense
heaven gives things, and wise people fled.

Huang and Ch'i left for Shang Mountain,
and these villagers were also never seen

again. Covering all trace of their flight,
the path they came on slowly grew over and

vanished. They worked hard tending fields
together, and come dusk, they all rested.

When mulberry and bamboo shade thickened,
planting time for beans and millet came.

Spring brought the silkworm's long thread,
and autumn harvests without taxes. There,

overgrown paths crossing back and forth,
roosters calling to the bark of dogs,

people used old-style bowls for ritual
and wore clothes long out of fashion. Kids

wandered at ease, singing. Old-timers
happily went around visiting friends.

Things coming into blossom promised mild
summer days, and bare trees sharp winds.

Without calendars to keep track, earth's
four seasons of themselves became years,

and happy, more than content, no one
worried over highbrow insights. A marvel

hidden away five hundred years, this
charmed land was discovered one morning,

but pure and impure spring from different
realms, so it soon returned to solitude.

Wandering in the world, who can fathom
what lies beyond its clamor and dust. O,

how I long to rise into thin air and
ride the wind in search of my own kind.

Untitled

Great men want the four seas. I've only
wanted old age to come unnoticed like

this. My family together in one place,
kids and grandkids looking after each

other still, I linger out mornings over
koto and wine, the winejar never dry.

My clothes a shambles, exhausting every
joy, I sleep late now, and nod off early.

Why live like all those fine men, hearts
stuffed with fire and ice to the end,

their hundred-year return to the grave
nothing but an empty path of ambition?

Written One Morning in the 5th Month, After Tai Chu-Pu's Poem

It's all an empty boat, oars dangling free,
but return goes on without end. The year

begins, and suddenly, in a moment's glance,
midyear stars come back around, bright

sun and moon bringing all things into such
abundance. North woods lush, blossoming,

rain falls in its season from hallowed
depths. Dawn opens. Summer breezes rise.

Has anyone come into this world without
leaving it? Life will always end. At home

in what lasts, I wait it out. A bent arm
my only pillow, I keep emptiness whole.

Move with change through rough and smooth,
and life's never up or down. If you see

how much height fills whatever you do,
why climb Hua or Sung, peaks of immortals?

UNTITLED

Days and months never take their time.
The four seasons keep bustling each other

away. Cold winds churn lifeless branches.
Fallen leaves cover long paths. We're

frail, crumbling with each turning year.
Our temples turn white early, and once

that bleached streamer's tucked into your
hair, the road ahead starts closing in.

This house is an inn awaiting travelers,
and I another guest leaving. All this

leaving and leaving – where will I ever
end up? My old home's on South Mountain.

ELEGY FOR MYSELF

It's the late-autumn pitch-tone *Wu-yi, Ting* year of the hare. The heavens are cold now, and the nights long. Geese pass, traveling south in desolate, windswept skies. Leaves turn yellow and fall. I, Master T'ao, will soon leave this inn awaiting travelers, and return forever to my native home. Everyone grieves. Mourning together, they've gathered here tonight for these farewell rites. They're making offerings to me: elegant foods and libations of crystalline wine. I look into their already blurred faces, listen to their voices blending away into silence.
Hu-ooo! Ai-tsai hu-ooo!

Boundless – this vast heap earth,
this bottomless heaven, how perfectly

boundless. And among ten thousand
things born of them, to find myself

a person somehow, though a person
fated from the beginning to poverty

alone, to those empty cups and bowls,
thin clothes against winter cold.

Even hauling water brought such joy,
and I sang under a load of firewood:

this life in brushwood-gate seclusion
kept my days and nights utterly full.

Spring and autumn following each other
away, there was always garden work –

some weeding here or hoeing there.
What I tended I harvested in plenty,

and to the pleasure of books, *koto*
strings added harmony and balance.

I'd sun in winter to keep warm,
and summers, bathe in cool streams.

Never working more than hard enough,
I kept my heart at ease always,

and whatever came, I rejoiced in all
heaven made of my hundred-year life.

Nothing more than this hundred-year
life – and still, people resent it.

Afraid they'll never make it big,
hoarding seasons, they clutch at

days, aching to be treasured alive
and long remembered in death. Alone,

alone and nothing like them, I've
always gone my own way. All their

esteem couldn't bring me honor, so
how can mud turn me black? Resolute

here in my little tumbledown house,
I swilled wine and scribbled poems.

Seeing what fate brings, our destiny
clear, who can live without concern?

But today, facing this final change,
I can't find anything to resent:

I lived a life long and, cherishing
solitude always, abundant. Now

old age draws to a close, what more
could I want? Hot and cold pass

away and away. And absence returns,
something utterly unlike presence.

My wife's family came this morning,
and friends hurried over tonight.

They'll take me out into the country,
bury me where the spirit can rest

easy. O dark journey. O desolate
grave, gate opening into the dark

unknown. An opulent coffin Huan's
disgrace, Yang's naked burial a joke,

it's empty – there's nothing in death
but the empty sorrows of distance.

Build no gravemound, plant no trees –
just let the days and months pass

away. I avoided it my whole life,
so why invite songs of praise now?

Life is deep trouble. And death,
why should death be anything less?

    Hu-ooo! Ai-tsai hu-ooo!

BURIAL SONGS

I

Whatever will live will die. I died
young, though not shortchanged by fate.

Last night I was like anyone else.
This morning I'm listed among ghosts.

The spirit thins away who knows where,
leaving a dry body inside hollow timber.

Looking for their father, my pampered
children cry. Friends touch me, sobbing.

But I'll never know gain and loss again,
or worry over good and evil. After

some thousand autumns or ten thousand
years, who knows honor from disgrace?

Of my time in the world, I only regret
drinking so often without enough wine.

2

I used to live without wine. Now my
cup's brimful – and for what? This

spring wine's crowned with foam,
but how will I ever taste it again?

Delicacies crowd the altar before me,
and at my side, those I love sob.

I speak – it's a mouth of silence.
I look – eyes of darkness. I slept

beneath high ceilings; now I'll stay
in a waste village of weeds. I'll

set out this morning, leaving our gate
behind, and never find my way back.

3

Boundless – in the boundless, weed-ridden
wastes, white poplars moan in the wind.

In bitter ninth-month frost, come to this
distant place – it's farewell. All four directions

empty, not a house in sight, looming
gravemounds peak and summit. Wind

moaning to itself in the branches here,
horses rear up, crying out toward heaven.

Once this dark house is all closed up,
day won't dawn again in a thousand years.

Day won't dawn again in a thousand years,
and what can all our wisdom do about it?

Those who were just here saying farewell
return to their separate homes. And though

my family may still grieve, the others
must be singing again by now. Once you're

dead and gone, what then? Trust yourself
to the mountainside. It will take you in.

Many of T'ao Ch'ien's lines echo passages in the classical texts. This adds a deep resonance to his clear, natural language. However, to avoid losing the poems in scholarship, only references that are essential to a poem's primary meaning are explained in these notes. For extensive commentaries on T'ao Ch'ien's work and scholarly translations of the complete collection, see James Hightower's *The Poetry of T'ao Ch'ien* (Oxford, 1970) and A.R. Davis's *T'ao Yüan-ming: His Works and Their Meaning* (Cambridge, 1983).

Page 14 CUP AND BOWL WERE EMPTY AS OFTEN AS YEN HUI'S: The first of several admiring allusions to Confucius's favorite disciple, Yen Hui, who is exemplified in *Analects* 6/11 and 11/19:

> The Master said: "How noble Hui is! To live in a meager lane with nothing to eat or drink but a little rice in a split-bamboo bowl and water in a gourd cup – no one else could bear such misery. But it doesn't even bother Hui. His joy never wavers. How noble Hui is!"
>
> The Master said: "Hui has nearly made it. He is often empty."

Yen Hui died young as a result of the constant hunger he endured while cultivating the Confucian Way.

WU-HUAI, KO-T'IEN: Sage rulers from China's legendary prehistory.

Page 17 CH'I: Universal breath or life-giving principle.

Page 18 LIU CH'AI-SANG: Liu I-min, former prefect of Ch'ai-sang, T'ao Ch'ien's home village. This friend of T'ao's had retired to Lu Mountain, where he entered the monastery Hui-yüan ran near T'ao's farm.

Page 19 DUST: Insubstantial worldly affairs.

Page 21 SOUTH MOUNTAIN: A symbolic renaming of Lu Mountain. Calling up such passages as "like the timelessness of South Mountain" in the *Classic of Poetry (Shih Ching,* 166/6), South Mountain came to have a kind of mythic stature as the embodiment of the elemental and timeless nature of the earth. It later became an important element of T'ao's poetic world.

Page 23 *KOTO:* This term, now adopted into English from Japanese, is used to translate *"ch'in"* and *"se,"* ancient stringed instruments which are the *koto*'s Chinese ancestors, and which Chinese poets used to accompany the chanting of their poems.

Page 25 *KUEI* YEAR OF THE HARE: 403. In the traditional dating system, each year was identified with a Stem *(Kuei)* and a Branch (hare). There are ten Celestial Stems and twelve Earthly Branches, which combine in a regular order so that the same combination recurs every sixty years.
SOUTHERN FIELDS: A name familiar from numerous pastoral poems in the *Classic of Poetry.*

FARMER LAUGHING AT CONFUCIUS: One of T'ao's favorite allusions, from *Analects* 18/7:

> Tzu-lu was traveling with Confucius and fell behind. Meeting an old man carrying a basket on the cane over his shoulder, he asked, "Have you seen the master pass by here?" The old man replied, "Your four limbs have never known work, and you can't tell the five grains apart. Who is it you call master?" At this, he planted his walking-stick and began pulling weeds.

Page 26 WORRY ABOUT THE WAY, NOT HUNGER: Confucius says this in *Analects* 15/32.

PASSERSBY NEVER STOP TO ASK THE WAY: A nice reversal of the respect accorded Confucius in line 2, this is another recurring allusion, refering to *Analects* 18/6, where the "river crossing" represents the Way through this "surging and swelling" world, which a sage masters:

> As Confucius passed by, Ch'ang-chü and Chieh-ni were in the field plowing together. He sent Tzu-lu to ask them about the river crossing. Ch'ang-chü said, "Who's that you're driving for?" Tzu-lu answered, "It's Confucius." "You mean Confucius of Lu?" "Yes." "Then he knows the river crossing well." Tzu-lu then asked Chieh-ni, but Chieh-ni replied, "And who are you?" "I am Chung Yu." "You mean Chung Yu who is a disciple of Confucius of Lu?" "Yes." "It's all surging and swelling. Everything under heaven is awash. And who's going to change it? To follow a man who's given up people – how could that ever compare to following one who's given up the world?" And folding earth back over seed, he went on working without pause.

Page 28   12TH MONTH, *KUEI* YEAR OF THE HARE: January 404. In the Chinese lunar calendar, the first day of the year corresponds to the beginning of spring. It falls on a different day every year, somewhere between late January and late February, so the 1st month corresponds roughly to February and the 12th month to January.

RESOLUTE IN PRIVATION: A virtue highly regarded and often cited by T'ao. Borrowed from *Analects* 15/2:

> In Ch'en, when supplies ran out, the disciples grew so weak they couldn't get to their feet. Tzu-lu, his anger apparent, asked, "So the worthy also suffer such privation?" "If you're worthy, you're resolute in privation," Confucius replied, "If you're small, you get swept away."

Page 29   HAN HSIN: Han Hsin (d. 196 B.C.) rose from humble beginnings to become a famous general who was instrumental in founding the Han Dynasty. At one point, when he was penniless and half-starved, a washerwoman fed him for nearly a month. He promised to repay her handsomely one day, which he did.

Page 32   This is a *fu* (prose-poem), hence its irregular form.
11TH MONTH, *YI* YEAR OF THE SNAKE: December 405.

Page 35   CHANT, SETTLING INTO MY BREATH: A Taoist method of harmonizing with the natural world.

Page 37   Virtually all of the poems in this book are *ku-shih* (ancient-style), with five characters per line. But this poem employs a four-character line in imitation of the form used in the *Classic of Poetry*. Its title and preface are also in *Classic of Poetry* form.

Page 38   YI RIVER: This passage, and the spring clothes in T'ao's preface, recall *Analects* 11/26, where Confucius asks four disciples to describe what they would do if they were given control of a state. After the first three had given unacceptable answers, the last disciple laid his *koto* aside and said: "In late spring, when the spring clothes are all made, I would go with five or six friends and six or seven servant-boys to bathe in the Yi River and enjoy the breeze at Rain Dance Altars, then return home chanting poetry." Confucius approved.

HUANG AND T'ANG: Huang Ti (reign 2698–2598 B.C.) and Yao (reign 2357–2255 B.C.) are legendary emperors from China's semi-mythical Golden Age.

Page 39   FORM, SHADOW, SPIRIT: T'ao Ch'ien seems to have invented this tripartite division.

Page 41   GREAT POTTER: According to myth, he creates the ten thousand things on his potter's wheel, which turns like the four seasons. Thus, he is the personification of change, earth's ongoing process of spontaneous self-creation.

HUMANS RANK WITH HEAVEN AND EARTH: Heaven, earth, and human are the Three Powers.

THREE EMPERORS: Legendary emperors from the Golden Age in China's prehistory.

P'ENG-TSU: In legend, China's longest living human.

Page 44   9/9: Holiday celebrated on the ninth day of the ninth lunar month.

Page 45   9TH MONTH, *KENG* YEAR OF THE DOG: October 410. CHÜ AND NI: Ch'ang-chü and Chieh-ni. See note to page 26.

Page 47   CONFUCIUS IN CH'EN: See note to page 28.

Page 48   SOUTH VILLAGE: Located somewhere in the immediate neighborhood of Hsün-yang/Ch'ai-sang, probably just south of Hsün-yang. It isn't clear why T'ao moved to South Village, or how long he stayed. Although he continued farming there, most of his friends were fellow scholar-officials – some still in government, some living as recluse-farmers.

CH'I-SITED: It was thought that the different features of a landscape determine the movement of *ch'i*, the universal breath. The best site for a house would be determined by a diviner who analyzed the local movements of *ch'i* by using a divining rod and a special type of astrological compass.

Page 50   SHAO: Shao P'ing was the Marquis of Tung-ling under the Ch'in Dynasty. But when the Han overthrew the Ch'in (206 B.C.), he was reduced to growing melons for a living.

Page 52   CHRYSANTHEMUMS: The petals of chrysanthemums were mixed with wine to make chrysanthemum wine, popularly believed to promote longevity. Chrysanthemums have always been identified with T'ao Ch'ien because of the central place they held in his poetic world.

Page 54 PINE: Because they are large, strong, and always green, pines were seen by the Chinese as the embodiment of permanence and constancy, a stoicism which perseveres under the harshest conditions.

Page 55 YEN: Yen Hui, Confucius's disciple. See note to page 14.
JUNG: Jung Ch'i-ch'i, an impoverished ninety-year-old man in chapter 1 of *Lieh Tzu,* whose sagely contentment with the wonder of life itself impressed Confucius.
NAKED BURIAL: Yang Wang-sun (1st c. B.C.) insisted on being buried naked so he could return to his true (natural) state.

Page 58 ISLAND OF IMMORTALS: P'eng-lai, located far out in the Eastern Sea.

Page 59 1ST MONTH, *HSIN* YEAR OF THE OX: February 401. This date is textually corrupt.
K'UN-LUN MOUNTAINS: A mythic range in the far west, associated with immortality because it is home to Hsi Wang Mu, queen of the immortals, who grows the peaches of immortality in her palace gardens. There is a formation in these mountains with the same name as the cliffs T'ao and his friends are looking at: Tseng Cliffs.

Page 62 SUNG AND CH'IAO: Ch'ih Sung-tzu and Wang Tzu-ch'iao, examples of immortals from legendary antiquity.

Page 63 6TH MONTH, *WU* YEAR OF THE HORSE: July 418.
TUNG-HU: Tung-hu Chi-tzu, a sage ruler said to have lived in the twenty-ninth century B.C., at the beginning of China's legendary Golden Age.

Page 65 9/9: Dominated by thoughts of mortality, this autumn festival is celebrated on the 9th day of the 9th lunar month because the word for "9" (*chiu*) is pronounced the same as the word meaning "long-lasting" or "long-living," hence *"ever and ever."* Chrysanthemum wine is especially associated with this holiday. There is a famous passage in the early biographies which is traditionally associated with this poem. It tells how Wang Hung (page 69), the provincial governor-general and T'ao's friend, happened by when T'ao was out sitting among the chrysanthemums. Wang had some wine with him, and the two of them ended up getting drunk together.

Page 67 THE CLASSIC OF MOUNTAINS AND SEAS: An ancient book of fantasy, which describes the mythic geography of ancient China and other nearby lands. From line 14, it's clear that T'ao is reading an illustrated edition of the book. TALES OF EMPEROR MU: An ancient book of historical fantasy, which describes the mythic journeys of Emperor Mu (d. 946 B.C.).

Page 68 CHA FESTIVAL: Ancient name for the *La* Festival, which in T'ao's time, fell on the last day of the lunar year. It was the first day of New Year festivities celebrating the arrival of spring.

Page 69 GOVERNOR WANG: Wang Hung, the provincial governor-general in Hsün-yang from 418–425 and a friend of T'ao's, admiring him for his wisdom and integrity as a recluse.

Page 71 ASKED THE WAY: See note to page 26. HUANG AND CH'I: The hermits Hsia Huang-lung and Ch'i li-chi.

Page 75 HUA OR SUNG: Two of China's five sacred mountains, often climbed by pilgrims.

Page 77 This poem uses the four-character *Classic of Poetry* line for its classical austerity.

PITCH-TONE *WU-YI:* There was a series of twelve standard pitch-pipes used in ancient music, and each pitch corresponded to one of the twelve months. *Wu-yi* corresponds to the 9th lunar month, or October.

TING YEAR OF THE HARE: 427.

Page 80　HUAN: Huan T'ui had such an extravagant coffin made for himself that it took over three years to build.

YANG: Yang Wang-sun. See note to page 55.

CPSIA information can be obtained
at www.ICGtesting.com
Printed in the USA
JSHW021713230122
22192JS00002B/7